Into the Woods

Written by
Stephen Rickard

Ransom

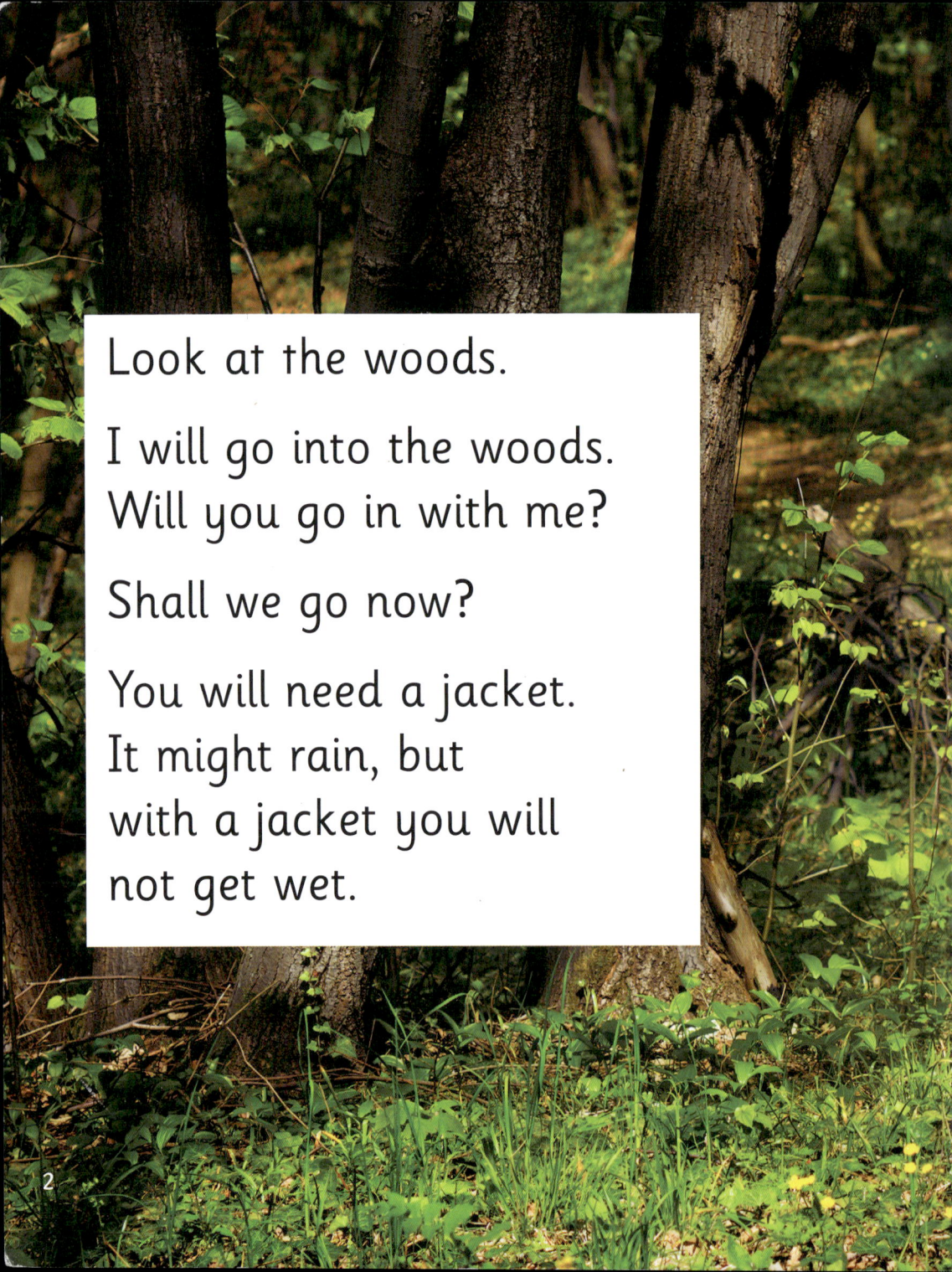

Look at the woods.

I will go into the woods.
Will you go in with me?

Shall we go now?

You will need a jacket.
It might rain, but
with a jacket you will
not get wet.

I can see a fox in the woods.

Can you see it?

Is it a fox or is it a vixen?

Look! It is a vixen with her cubs. She has a litter of six cubs.

She waits with her six cubs as they run and fight.

Then they will all go back to the den.

Can you see an owl
in the woods?

Owls are hard to see.
But we can see them
if we look hard.

This owl is looking
down at us.

This owl will wait for the night.

Then it will look for food.

Can you hear an owl hoot at night?

You can see a lot in the woods,
if you wait and look.

Will you visit with me again
in a week?